JUMPING JACK

JUMPING JACK

Keith Howden

PENNILESS PRESS PUBLICATIONS

Published by

Penniless Press Publications 2022

Keith Howden

ISBN 978-1-913144-40-1

Cover: Keith Howden

Contents

Serve me now, arcane and furtive
Will-o'- the Wisp, ephemeral in illusion's
recondite namings. Obey me, *Spunkie*,
move mettlesome to my fen. Know me, *Elf-fire*,
malignant imp of defects and disease,
bowman of elf-bolts. Be at my side
Bog-fire, Walk-flame, Friar's Lanthorn,
Goodfellow's bad brother, *Puck* in
dirt's disguise. Assist me, debauched
and fire baptised, fetch your corruption
to the law's votaries. Abet me, hobgoblin
conjuror whose winking leads
to the Devil's night club. Come learned to me
as *Ignis Fatuus*, come ignorant as *Fool's Fire*.
Androgynous and hermaphrodite
Jack o' Lantern, Peg o' Lantern, fetch me
fugitive immortality, lend your spontaneous
combustion from decay, your rot's skidding
phosphorescence. Vouchsafe me that imposture
safety that urges fools astray. Be *Joan the Wad*.
Squat sprite in the future's languages
of pixels on a screen. Be my servant
Soul Gnome in your salamander planet,
be *Jack the Lad*, be *Jack in the Green*,
be *Jumping Jack* in a quicksilver cosmos
of arsenic, ammonia and brimstone. Be my
necrotic juggler, conjure your waxy and
poisonous valency to shape the warlock light
the simple fear as the unfostered souls
of stillborn children lost between
Heaven's bulb and the Inferno's flame.

All my Dead Uncles

1.

'All Your dead Uncles.' Their images beamed,
Albert and Walter, James and John and Henry,
from sepia photographs unframed,
a cracked and yellowing rosary
fixed by shrivelled sellotape, forming
a rank on George's mirror. Puisieux and Serre.
Fell on the Somme. I knew the chiselling
of names in gilded stone: the year,
nineteen sixteen: a pigeon-woman's songs.
But better this, their soiled, immutable
immortality, their frozen starings
from the etched mirror, their suitable
patriotism. Bullet-belted, drawn
in khaki smiles and not that long from falling,
Albert and Henry, Walter, James and John
smiling with not much time for smiling.
'A hole big as an egg-cup in his head,
young Walter died in my arms.' George moved
in landscapes where his khaki youth had stayed
and my dead Uncles of his memory survived.
Water was running high. From George's, we
could hear the upstream rumble of the weir
marching its froth battalions endlessly
in regiments through the winter air.

2.

In George's house at the spluttering weir,
stuck to the mirror hanging at a lean,
Albert and Henry, James and John and Walter,

all my dead Uncles marched a garden scene
etched into glass. In a thin cartoon,
parasol girls kept eternal guard,
hollyhock lances speared a gilded sun
and in unlikely trees an unlikely bird
carolled a scratch. Two symmetrical
cellophane butterflies on suckers clung
to a reflecting sky. 'That mirror's all
I ever kept of what he left me. Young
Walter loved it. Look at it – a poem in
itself.' George boasted with no diffidence,
offering his aesthetic implication
as something I was sure to countenance.
The pigeon-woman's croon, the bloody Somme,
Walter and Henry, James and John and Albert
were emblems impotent to guard or damn
his mirror's mediocre tact and art.
The river wheeling woundedly and slow
carried detritus, scum making its march
in broken ranks. High water had bombed through
earlier, to storm the bridge's arch.
George dragged my childhood out of humdrum,
constructing khaki myths for my retrieve:
Puisieux, Serre, the trenches and the grim
mess of their ends. 'All bloody five
dead in a week. Young Walter looked like you.
Died in my arms.' In my mind's shambles,
George's mirror fossils their bravado
and permanence, all my dead Uncles.

3.

Cousin Tom's mimicry: 'Poor Walter died.
And Henry, Albert, John and James…'
With his thin face and frame, he imitated

9

George's stump walk and psalmodies.
Without a cap, he hinted George's, wore
invisibly the stained fag drooping slack
on George's lip. 'Piss Puisieux and Serre.
bugger his Somme.' Tom put his mark
on names I'd learned as rosary of a cult
more sensitive, the trench orison
that Tom, ungulled, heard only as the fault
in scratches of a broken gramophone.
Later, with George near the swollen river,
Albert and Henry, James, John, Walter all
marched broken between us. Tom's mirror
tainted their image, ordered our squall.
In George's garden by the weir, we quarrelled
where, at our side, sheathed leaves of lilac
strained to a disappointing spring. A cold
April morning saluted a fleck
of sun in grey sky. In the wet meadows
beyond the weir the weak light flared its sour
illumination and the white asbestos
of football stands was briefly golden. 'Your
sod of a cousin Tom's done this,' George said,
marshalling yet again John, James and Henry
Albert and young Walter, egg-cup holed,
all my dead Uncles marching khaki,
parading the river's swill downstream.
Above, the weir churned its April spate
in regiments of froth, their column
broken by mortar winds along the straight.

4.

'Caught anything?' George was loading
battles and blood into his query.
Wilf, oil-skinned, had caught George descending

to stall his fishing in the river bay.
Much comradeship involved the lower air.
'Wilf fought in France,' George said. I'd known.
We turned towards the splutter of the weir.
Wilf had progressed, was George's implication
into the dry, self-gratifying peace-
ful whims of age, while he had stayed to choose
politics' battleground. 'They call this place
Moscow because of me.' The empty phrase
cracked acres of time. I'd heard his same
expression years ago, a boastful paean
before the photographs and, mocking him,
Tom had stabbed accurately at his tone
and names I'd held as sentimental creed.
Later, I watched George posture, stand
by the rails of the weir as he proposed
himself, when young, dead Walter's friend -
He looked like you do now - Albert and James,
Henry and John, grey hair against grey sky.
Tom had been right to stab. 'They call this place
Moscow because of me.' My sympathy
for him had shrivelled. Puisieux and Serre
the pigeon-woman's songs, the Somme,
Albert and Henry, James and John and Walter:
George marshalled an appeal but it was time
to raise them in a morning's colder light.
'Caught anything?' I mocked his charlatan
postures with Wilf. Tom had been right
to stab. George spun deflated for me then.

5.

Fitful sun pecking the gilded grooves
of Puisieux and Serre, Fell on the Somme,
lit pigeons on the graveyard's drives

and the stump Cenotaph. Albert and John,
Henry, Walter, James: George traced the stone
East Lancashires. 'Young Walter looked
like you.' The pigeon-woman's croon
was with me but George had tracked
to nearer things. 'Tom Morton's made a mess.
One bloody woman and he's winded.
A pig's ear of a marriage.' Time to recognise
an old man anxious to be reminded
by any blandishment at my disposal
that he had stayed the four years of a war
and more than Tom had had his fill
of women. 'When we were over there
we didn't go without.' Scum platoons
formed ranks along the river's shelf,
swilled slowly down in punk battalions,
and open order, passing the Cenotaph,
the weir's conscripted infantry,
detritus bubbles parading in their
regiments on the move, a bladder army.
khaki impostures on the water.

'Apres la guerre finee
Soldiers Anglais partee,
Beaucoup M'amselles dans la family way.
Apres la guerre pitee......'

I hawked the pigeon-woman's song and he
took it with savour. With it, I urged mistake
for flattery but offered a trenched mockery
without commitment. If he chose to look
no further than surface geography,
it gestured what he had wanted, lands
to conjure adulation. 'When you try,
you're the only one who understands.'

12

Sudden sunlight flecked the graves,
regilding momentarily his stone
East Lancashires, their fading names,
Albert and Henry, Walter James and John.

6.

The river marching slow in single shots,
grey water lapping the military weir,
attrition weather scorched the bankside flats,
trenching the waterline. A squad of star-
lings squabbled over bread. George lay
under the butterflies of Walter's mirror
necropolis, remaking loonily
his khaki myths. The pigeon-woman's wraith
crooned for him there, spilling the words
that carried for him the flux memory
of my dead Uncles, the bauble-lads
of Puisieux and Serre: Albert and Henry,
James and John, relentless as the scums
he told them: Walter who never died -
he looked like you do now - reclaimed his arms,
a hole big as en egg-cup in his head.
The river's sluggish channel paced his mind.
Stagnant detritus had overpiled
in spawny clumps. Capricious wind
flirted the clusters upstream. Then a shrivelled
and sudden, contorted anger marked
his mood. He jerked to mouth accusingly –
'Henry and Walter, James and John and Albert –'
marshalled their memory to damn me.
'I was your friend. Young Walter looked like you.
Tom Morton made us enemies, the bastard.'
Then sank to ride the river's sluggish flow
towards them, old and exhausted.

7.

In George's house by the spluttering weir,
stuck to his mirror, hanging at a lean,
six photographs. East Lancashire,
he'd written on each one. Crinoline
ladies, hollyhocks, that sharp bird among
the etched trees still commanded the frame
and of the khaki images that clung,
we carried out the last. Five chiselled names
I knew in polished stone, but knew this grander,
sepia deathlessness. Six cracked and faded
photographs had petrified a bland or
wondering, glazed but still unjaded
patriotism. Bullet-belted, shrined
in thin and khaki smiles, not far from falling,
unthinking, ignorant and blind,
five smiled with not much time for smiling.
The river sliding downstream, dully,
a light wind rippling in clearer patches,
cumbersome regiments of froth moved slowly
bridgeward, veered in gusts between the houses.
Bushed and intricate, contorted squads
slithered the river's central path,
swilled slowly downstream, punk armadas
under sunshine fading, past the Cenotaph.
I watched them drop the last of George away,
counted nine mourners, heard intoned,
with not much vigour, hope or urgency
words he rejected, watched them hymn the God
he'd never found. Earth that should have smacked
ritually at his coffin was a pinch
of finest to be found. With decency and tact
they killed what he had been. Judged to the inch,

we posted him respectably away.
I had mixed feelings for him then, played games
with hidden grief, added in mockery
another to those five chiselled names.

8.

On the stump Cenotaph's architectures
a generation too removed for pity
scrawled its bewilderments. Dead fusiliers
wore camouflage where obscene graffiti
saluted cruder loves and posturings
than theirs. From fluted pillars, pigeons
at their dung trades grouted the chisellings,
turning to shit my Uncles' gilded runes.
The weir in winter flood, its boom
built bubble monuments, toppling the spate
into a floodgate swill, landscaped a Somme
of scum exhaustion labouring the flat.
Daily and loonily she limped the rail
beside the Cenotaph, distributing
manna in pinches. Around her, a swell
of bucking pigeons scrummed to her song.
She threw a spray of crumbs, hauling a drogue
of hopelessness in her bewildered rave,
cursing the birds she fed, a monologue
that hymned her crazy no-man's land of love.
And there, beneath the Cenotaph, George spun
back in those silted chisellings that will
embalm and emblemise him better than
emotion for the men they name. Yet still,
let me recount them, all my dead Uncles, James,
Albert and Henry, John, Walter who died –
He looked like you do now – in George's arms,
a hole big as an egg-cup in his head.

Barley Top

1.

I wear them, ranting bastards,
my blood forebears, children
of unforgiving creeds,
acid within their moor. Malign

religioned as their weather,
abrasive as their hinterland's
hostility, liming to nurture
a bitter soil. Arthritic minds

raised chapels, rheum endowed
harmoniums groaning a Zion
complicit with their wound,
foetal within their landscape's pain

of names rotted to debris,
their walls' atavism, their intake's
compliant apostasy.
We wear implicit the impress

of maps transmitted through
long generations to compel
blood's shared imbroglio
with the lineaments of our fell.

No logic nominates the ground
or sanctifies the contour's stain.
To understand the wound
is not to heal the pain

2.

I rant them, catechism,
those garble citadels of the moor,
names conjured in the prism
of a wry religion's grandeur.

Grime, Limers, Bullion:
Myrtle Earth, Rush Candle, Mean Hey:
Jericho, Noah, Zion
Egypt: Slate Pits, Folly.

I name them, blackened bibles
of intake's apostasy,
assume their gibber syllables
in a rammel psalmody.

Ratten, Feist End, Gibbet:
Nouch, Lench, Gorple, Doal,
White Riding: Old Nick, Boggart:
Wormden, Bleakholt, Bone Hole.

I chant their dearth oblation,
the fossil babels of the fells,
seized in their weather's incantation,
germane within their vowels.

Nut Shaw, Delph Brink, Coppy:
Mary's Chair, Tolerance, Love Clough:
Horsehold, Whittle, White Kink, Cronkie,
Windy Gate, Rake Head, Nab Rough.

17

I tell their gabble rosary,
blab chapels of that plangent zeal,
intone their plainsong irony,
barren and evangelical.

Famine Ridge, Further, Windy Harbour,
Wreck Beds, Bleak House, Stone Crop:
Slack Myres, Wet Head: Hard Labour,
Needless, Poverty, Barley Top.

3.

Who names the moor?
    'I,' said the drover.
'In Bastard Clough, through Sod's Toll, at Hard Labour,
christen the salt's power.'

Who psalms the moor?
    'I,' said the curlew.
'At Love Clough, on Tolerance, over Sweet and Mellow,
chant the salt lanes below.'

Who pays the moor?
    'I,' said the drunkard.
'Through Swiggit, round Ale Corner, in Tosspot's Yard,
salt tickles the landlord.'

Who knows the moor?
    'I,' said the pony.
'Up Skidders' Bank, on Whip Hill, down Stumble Valley,
lugging the salt's economy.'

Who clothes the moor?
    'I,' said the grass.
'By Meadow Head, in Horsehold, under Goodshaws,
ripped by the salt's traverse.'

Who cheats the moor?
    'I,' said the shrine.
'At Jesus Wept, at Mary's Chair, across Zion,
concealing salt's religion.'

Who shapes the moor?
    'I,' said the track.
'From Rake Head, over Slate Pits, at High Turnpike,
with salt wounding my back.'

Who sweeps the moor?
    'I,' said the rain.
'Down Foul Syke, down Deep Ditch, down Filthy Drain,
 salt to salt the waters run.'

Who shrives the moor?
    'I,' said the whip.
'From Jericho, round Hades, up Hell's Rip,
speaking salt's ownership.'

Who rules the moor?
    'I,' said money.
'Without me, Famine Ridge, Bleak House, Poverty,
salt worthless, the shrines empty.'

4.

Came to the ruined, dry-walled farm
in one of the barren folds of the hill,
its rafters raking the wind, its barn
vanished, but on the spanning lintel, still

crudely but deeply chiseled was the name
I'd sought, the legend, *Barley Top*. It crooned
of my grandfathers' boyhoods, wasted time,
life undernourished on infertile ground.

Even now, though rushes and bog-tufts spread
and vaulted walls and dragged aside the door,
a different, limier green betrayed
land lost by and recaptured by the moor.

I thought of those old builders, the sour land
desolate, unpropitious to their hope.
The name declared an optimism and
sheep they must have kept, but *Barley Top*

spoke languages of pathos, the frail nimbus
of stillborn dream, and *Barley Top* broken,
crumbling at the moor's relentlessness,
was every foundered hope for me then.

Wind trapped and blundering among the stone
took me to times that solitary, wry,
my grandfathers acknowledged as their own,
shoeless before the turning century.

5.

My father's father's feral
apocrypha rolled his father's
mage annexation of the fell.
Sick sheep, the halt ram Topaz

barking in frost, the black mule
Benjamin staggering lame
from winter saltways. His oracle
voices roared millennium.

a benign weather's imminence,
while snow suckled the bacon blots
of his flock's abortions and bones
buckled in rain. The milk goats

drooped shrivel tits. Winter strangled
and wind boiled the grasses
where beltane bracken brindled.
A delivery of voices

pronounced that place's site,
which slab to lay, the solemn grain
of rafters: where communion light
should hole the walls, each stone

a mad *Hallelujah,* every slate
a cracked *Amen.* Deaf hearing learnt
the stars' clattering turn, blind sight
swung angels on his firmament

to garrison sunset, tied tongue
catechised clouds. Another
delivery of voices slung
anarchic bulletins to blather

that place's name. The maul
possessed his chisel and something
arcane within the lintel
compelled his ouija christening

of *Barley Top*. What wry
epistemologies or hopes
conjured that alphabet queerly
occult in his disease?

Lime failed his intake ventures.
Flocks rotted. Halt Topaz died
and the mad currency of voices
crashed on within his head

No logic nominates that ground
or sanctifies his contour's stain.
To understand the wound
is not to heal the pain.

6.

Greenteeth. They named their horror.
The witch fell's schism
bred him their moor's familiar,
its instinct ectoplasm.

Winter carcasses bared his tooth,
ghost wethers bleated his hymns.
Black birds chanted him. *Greenteeth*
spun inchoate in their names.

His holt was stinking water.
They met his boggart gloss
in methane alleys, his cadaver
loom in the amorphousness

of mist. Scared genets skittered
the echoes haunting gullies
where euphemism slithered
syllables of his alias.

The Irish carving canals
felt him shudder the spade's plunge,
wince at the pick. In candle tunnels
heard the shibboleth revenge

of dialect name their fear.
Semantic in sour soil, he hung
cognate in sounds, his spectre
colloidal in their mouthing.

Greenteeth. In gnostic chapels,
Rechabite roarings congealed
his darker doctrines. Taradiddles
maimed their psalms. Heresy cawed

in anthems. A coven drum
tumped Amen. Hallelujahs spat
carrion to gorge the phantom
hermetic in the pulpit.

7.

They claimed the moor for neighbour, etched their farms
- *Rake Head, Windy Harbour* - in acid parishes
where vision led. Names gaunt with truth dissenting
the seasons' rituals, crude as wind ranting
its barren testaments. Faith's harbingers, they preached
labour's utilitarian religion.

Trespassed their neighbour's cloisters, sacked his shrines
- *Nut Shaw, Barley Top* - where they commanded
walls built to stem or swerve his sour recoil.
Syllables relevant as famine, each name
the thing it was, security against
the moor's revenges. They staked his land their own.

These were their lime evangelism's chapels
- *Stone Fold, Wet head* - faith's proper prisons,
sites christened by the land's austerity.
With pulpit vowels, hallelujah consonants
denied the moor's religion, raised their psalms
apostate in their neighbour's mysteries.

Bibles of picks and ploughs, they consecrated
- *Old Barn, New Barn* - names nodding at hunger.
From laagered missions, won among the infidel
intake some scattered gestures of conversion.
Nothing recanted. No miracle redeemed
indigenous atheism in the grass.

The bald moor holds them now. The leper stations
- *Cronkie, White Riding* - where vision foundered
stand sepulchres to that dead neighbourhood
gospelled in names. Nobody stayed. No labour
prospered to breach the moor's truth. Nothing appeased
a god dissolved in different sacraments.

8.

I map my father's Uncle,
quarryman, scraping the bone
of moor, who heard the rankle
instinct in its skeleton

and met its spectre mason,
a phantom his memory wrenched
from some diorama frisson
nightly shadowing his bed.

His transoms fractured, his doors'
cartilage buckled, their frames
contorted by the insidious
ratchet of the moor's carapace.

Two names haunted his lodge:
Beelzebub, Ichabod.
Portent in his sortilege
casting of runes foretold

malevolence underground,
a cockatrice, milesian
muscling of stone, earth's wound
opening for the millennium

of Revelation's Six Six Six,
Apocalypse's magma
pulse of the new basilisk
unfossiled, beating Omega.

His jambs skewed. Lintels henged
inimical. The gradient rolled
the moor's frame in a scavenged
shamble to charnel his field.

Stone shocked his door's bastion.
The mole instinct of spoil
gnawed his tilth. He heard *Abaddon*
breathing skulls to his wall.

No logic nominates his ground
or sanctifies his quarry stain.
Geologies of his wound
abjure his map of pain.

9.

I wear him narrow minded,
my father's father, exile
from Barley Top, whose toad
So be it, Lord, whose servile

Amen, I early learned
were fox propitiation
of his Omerta godhead,
whose *Hallelujah* equation

meant Heaven's ambush wrath
averted. Never the squander
barkings of a laudation faith
but gold return for his vendetta

redeemer, one equally engrossed,
his mafia Jehovah,
by acquisition, cash and lust.
The moor's witch anathema

claimed him, stirred apostate,
congealing his litanies,
vital and unregenerate,
usurped the Hebrew pieties.

renting his pew. A religion
barren as stone, severe
as hunger fermented his bone.
Barley Top clawed his fervour.

Its Eden anthems hauled him
in the years he blasted stone,
still acolyte of its prism
altar, its bleak persuasion.

Now trucks in crippled phalanxes,
testudo at the ginny's head,
emblem the moor's spent industries,
correlative of the cracked

apocrypha of his faith.
Lost intake strangles the slope.
Wind wrangles the rafter teeth,
unbuilds the walls of *Barley Top*.

10.

Listen: rearing into hills
the road hymns release
from prison terraces,
promising somewhere else.

It leans a Jacob's ladder
to scale the encroaching moor
where tankers, fonts sour
with acid, clatter under

the fell's scowl. Lorries altared
with quarrying's process rattle
the day's matins, haul
out of shadow, shuttle trade

to further highways.
A changed prospect assembles
another landscape's walls
and different geographies.

Listen: the whining vehicles
of choirs traffic epistles
under the moor's oracles,
promising somewhere else.

Bladdering Whitsun's banners,
infidel wind shudders
the flexible architectures
of Zion where the boxed gears

of hymns grind parables
contesting sceptical contours.
A sermon's engine stutters
the road to Christian bliss.

Prayers broker a faith
alien to the moorhead's
agnosticism. The summit breeds
maps for belief's untruth.

Riding the landscape's quarrel,
the road makes manifest
different distances. Christ
inhabits the wind's swell

of blustering banners where
the tankers' daily religion
corrodes. The land's skin
is scored with acid: the moor

is yearly burned: the fells
daily quarried. The road's census
tells only its traffic's use,
promising nowhere else.

11.

Brash in the moor's economy,
their outpost's arcane scrape
scratches a stone. Its irony
mocks their labour. *Barley Top.*

I wear that cipher name,
my witch emblem of the fells
where wind charnels a scheme
of supine stone. The lintel's

menhir mumbles the chisel's
runing, a wryness that honed
my father's father's parables
of hope dissolved in acid ground.

Now bog-cotton and rushes burn
its hearths, bracken panels the door,
lime's fossil taint runs stubborn
in intake garbled by the moor.

the name survives, its pathos
- faith's impotent contour
in the moor's relentlessness -
encodes their leper tenure.

Wind blundering the grass
conjures with bones. I mourn
my father's father, shoeless
under the century's turn.

12.

I chart a ribald pentecost
to map my father. I am
the child beside him, late in frost
allotments, the moon chromium

with cold, the path's steel tempered
to tuning fork, ringing my frisson
footsteps in tensile air. Then seized
on rigid rods, in iron

equipoise, I saw those planet
skulls of chrysanthemums, blight
icon worlds, iced element
of nowhere, their frozen orbit

stemmed higher than my breath
clouding in cold. Moon was
a brittle paleolith.
In that white starlessness,

snow spun a wafer spectrum
of crumbled glass. But nebular
and insensible, that system
burst its void paternoster

to sear my knowing. No faith
survived that existential kiss
of golem otherness, unbirth
of all pathetic fallacies.

Moon leered that orrery,
poising each automaton head
in nowhere's primal nullity.
Till then, no miracle released

the codes of emptiness whose curse,
green in my gut, spoke parable
of nothing's stoic universe,
of being's ishmael babel.

From them, we mortared chapels
in different stone. For him,
the moor's sour canticles,
scrape intake's whining psalm,

the hill's enigma prism,
wore god's undoubted signature.
Two crossed sticks' barbarism
nailed his profoundest rapture.

I map that frost damascus,
still coldly absolute,
my gethsemane dogmas
of the sprit's vacuum transit.

13.

I carve it with words' maul,
that mapping : *Barley Top* : redeem
the page's arcane lintel
with its ouija autism.

I map its prison landscapes,
its prisms of ancestry,
its esemplastic equipoise
in love's commodity.

Barley Top shapes my deity,
unfolds the castrate parables
of intake, the geld psalmody
in rank upland's syllables,

flares boggart and ineffable
in the mind's methane alleys, looms
amorphous in blood's garble
nothing. Its anarchisms

poise the apostate equation
congealed in ruin's metaphor
that spayed us the fell's children,
erotic eunuchs of the moor.

I map myself, bone puppet
of that taint blight whose stigma
revels in flesh's state,
ingrains the witch anathema,

eidetic and embedded in
the landscape's lie : articulate,
ferments in skin's palatinate
internecine, *Barley Top's* stain

usurping the litanies
renting my flesh. I know that mantis
whose numen is to fuse
nothing's barren enigmas.

I carve the icon index
occult within its avatars,
the infibulating paradox
hermetic in our altars.

Incidents on the Moor

1. Joe Anderson

What witnesses? I call the ballock sun,
its banded light bounced from the canal fence
to testify. The randy cats sunning on
brown linoleum hold telling evidence.
Witnessing what? Joe Anderson among
his hunks of ripe and rotten meat to breed
maggots for fishing where, too long
confined, the particles explode
in iridescence, new bluebottles boom
and splinter in confusion at the light,
clouding the level sunshine of the room.
Do I subpoena witnesses to that?
Joe moved with a superb dexterity,
stalked bluebottles, cupping his hand
pelota-shape, to strike out suddenly
and hold them in his palm docile and stunned.
What witnesses? I call the willow-herb
raping the corrugated outhouse roof.
The cats at randy picnic in the yard,
if they had time, would offer certain proof.
Witnessing what? Dexterously he wound,
holding them unconscious and unbroken,
a hair about them. To the other end
he used to tie a small and banal slogan.
On summer days the layered air was hung
with his late captives and their droning weight.
Each hauled its trite but miracle drogue
through spaces of the still and even light.
Guinness is Good or Beer is Best was all
that he, Your Worship, managed in that sphere,

less sharp in mind than in that physical
talent he brought perfected from nowhere.
What witnesses? I call the ballock sun
to testify. I call the randy cats,
the raping willow-herb, Joe Anderson.
Dare I subpoena witnesses to that?
It was another climate and that sun
went black. The randy cats defected. Rusts
blighted the willow-herb. The bannered drone
of flies is hypothetical and wastes
in my mind's prairies. Joe Anderson
cancered and died. The defence rests.

2. Spring Song

Wakening spring's assault and psalter,
larks rang their bursting business of the fell,
plovers possessed a pulsing sun, the air
held singing distances for new growth's swell.
It was that day, crest piled on crest,
nascent earth's anthem for the spring,
with spearing tendrils of fine grass
and pent life driving, burgeoning.
The road, in the pulse of sun achieved
light's asphalt distances and realms of air,
married a trumpet light, the nuptial wind
swung rituals in aisles of looping wire.
That fullness burgeoned to a bleak excess.
A black discordancy, a breaking,
waited to breach the sun's largesse,
remap the contours of emergent spring.

3. Incident on the moor

Boys found, bird nesting on the April moor,
near where we lay, a hand-grenade.
Larks rose and fell. We heard the squeal of fear,
the dull explosion's echo. Someone 'Dead,'
was shouting on the ridge. And then, the men
returning with the body and the wastrel
soaring larks upthrust in spring's momen-
tum, charred moor grass stinking in my nostril.
Above us, suddenly where we lay,
black larks cascaded, climbing broken air
in flights unconsummated over the boy
with blown-off hands. And then that other,
that demon boy, white-legged, long-shorted howled
along the ridge. Larks black as time, but older,
fiercer than spring's explosion, held
his cry in scorn. Over the rim of the moor
we saw him lurch. 'Dead,' he was shouting.
Black-haired, he wore thick glasses and larks hung
black at his head, charred grass detonating
black at his feet. 'Dead,' he was shouting.

4. Love Song

It was that living day of the fell's grace,
the burst moor's celebration of the spring,
with spearing tendrils of fine grass,
a pent life nascent, burgeoning.
'Tell me about Joe Anderson,' she said.
I might have told the sun, its light
dancing in sibilants of acid
in half-litre beakers, the jewelled weight
of flies towing the miracle drogues
of Beer is Best and Guinness is Good.

36

I might have told the catalogues
of what she meant to me. I never did.
His hair was black, that demon boy. He wore
bottle-bottom glasses. Black larks hung
about his head and the charred moor
exploded at his feet. 'Dead,' he was shouting
I might have told the willow-herb's decay.
'Tell me about Joe Anderson,' she said.
I might have told the cats, maybe imply
that I loved her. I never did.

5. Equipoise.

1.

Boys hunting curlew eggs were moving where
remnants of ammunition dumps lie on
the fell's flank. We heard the dull explosion.
In that disastrous telling, he comes over
the ridge of the moor, my golem. He wears
the shock of his black hair, those thick-lensed
bottle glasses. 'Dead,' he is shouting 'Dead.'
He is more and less than human. He carries,
outside my understanding, some echo of the moor's
past mystery. Something arcane and mordant
comes with him. Black larks are crescent
about him where the explosion's rumours
shudder the pendulum. 'Dead. He's blown
his bloody hands off.' His bottle-lenses
gleam in an impossible light, burnt grasses
explode unreal in that manifestation
of the buried primitive, the witch knowing.
I remember running through nascent bracken
to The World's End's white isolation.
I recall my impatient waiting and shouting,

37

an urgent searching for some alarm
until the door was opened and my reason
half-understood by a sleepy young woman
in a black dress, who raises her white arm
in sunlight. And then the telephone
that brought an ambulance. Men stretchered down
the body from the moor, lurched through uneven
and tussocked grasses. I have no vision
throughout that time, of the black-haired boy.
He fills no space, might never have existed
except as some spectral fragment shaped
by the moor's numinous unreality.
I have carried his phantom presence,
punk priest of an otherness, febrile,
Lazarus in that explosion's quarrel
with the pendulum's normalities....

2.

The white car, still warm bonneted, was all
the car park held. I guessed its driver
the woman in broken light beside the bar.
'Ellen's in charge,' she said. 'Agnes is still...
that accident with the car...' Somewhere
there was a shift in the air's geographies
and Ellen stood behind the bar. Memories
came with her. I knew I had known her before.
There was a scuttering of claws on mesh.
I turned to see the monkey scraping the cage.
in the window bay that overlooked the ridge.
'Watch out for him,' the woman said. 'Agnes
hates him. He's always trying to bite.'
'We got Rufus,' Ellen said, 'after the parrot.
Somebody opened the cage and let it out.
We searched the moor. Dead when we found it.'

38

Black dressed, she returned a polished glass
and her pose, her uplifted arm, broke memory,
drove recollection back into that day
of the hand-grenade's explosion, the chaos
of larks, the enduring echo of 'Dead.'
I knew again that I had known her before.
I had seen soldiers quartering the moor,
their khaki ghosts a memory as they moved
now visible through the bay. Ellen grimaced.
'The ammunition dumps again.' 'At least
there's nobody hurt,' my fellow guest
seemed anxious to intrude and be included.
'I remember one being killed.' The limbo
of that old death consumed my mind,
shifted strongly through me. Ellen too moved
in memory. 'That's a long time ago.
I was courting then.' She twisted to review
her well-used plainness in the bar's mirror.
'I can remember sliding to get down here,
to phone and call the ambulance.' The screw
of Ellen's face was wry and unbelieving.
'There was no telephone then. You couldn't -
not from here. Things might be different
if you had....'

3.

'You couldn't have phoned from here.' There seemed
a deliberate antagonism in Ellen's
rebuttal of what I believed the prescience
of my memory. Not far away, outside,
without reference to the present, the fell
was bucking spring and I recalled the icon
stench of the moor, the larks in
fierce celebration, the nascent festival

of the year's businesses. Gaunt poles assaulted
the pub's white ride, bright water's psalters
ran whisky-gold over millstone stairs
and that enduring, griping memory spawned
the exploding grenade. A lost time's urgency
knew my lungburst down nascent bracken
to batter at the pub's locked door and then
its slow, complex opening, its emery
scrape on rough stone. And she was there,
the girl in a black dress, her white arm raised.
I remembered the zebra of sunlight and shade
invading the room, while behind the bar,
brindling among the bottles and turning
liquor to tortoiseshell, light's flint exploded
in inverted gin. Ellen beside me said,
'You couldn't have phoned from here….'

4.

'You couldn't have phoned from here,' she said.
How could I be wrong? That day's incident
had lived and burned in me and no recant
was possible. That boy, long-shorted,
white spindle legs and bottle-bottom glasses,
that howling of 'Dead' bursting to breach
the rim of the moor, that hurtle to reach
the white pub below. That, nothing could erase.
'You couldn't have phoned from here.' There was
a yearning for some otherness in her voice,
something unreachable in her response,
a lost fulfilment. I could only guess.
Leaving, I passed the monkey's cage. 'Watch him,'
the woman said. 'Agnes wants him gone
she says he bites.' 'I've every reason
to remember,' Ellen insisted. 'At that time

40

I was expecting a call. She couldn't ring.
There was no phone.' Outside the door,
my own ghost waited, haunting the moor,
Black-haired he waited. 'Dead' he was shouting.

6. Photograph

1.

I'd seen it before. I remembered it
casually passed around, some time when
it hardly mattered. Even by then,
it was the faded relic of a night,
an end of season dinner somewhere
expensive on the moor, and I'd forgotten
its existence until that later evening when
its twin appeared enlarged, its register
of realities revealed and dredged
untarnished from the album's open
neutrality. Madeleine was with me then
and she had often seemed concerned
that this was an image she believed had been
concealed deliberately from her……

2.

…and now, enlarged and glossier
more tellingly preserved, pristine
from the book's impartial imprisonment,
it emerged, a significant oracle,
to tell the treachery and betrayal
of that time, magnificently resonant
of our intrigues. In its intensification,
and through that undamaged gloss,
its sharpness uncovered in each of us,

41

almost a Dorian Gray detection,
things hidden, not solely from each other
but from ourselves, of which I'd had no sense
before: things that, on the evidence
of its diminished predecessor,
none of us would have known. In this
I came off badly and whatever
the multiplication of gesture
and expression had been, so far as
Agnes then mattered, this new gloss
lit meanings in my eyes I might explain
to myself but would never have shown
before the others, or made so obvious
as to be plain even to Madeleine's
undoubted innocence. It might have led her
to doubt my previous reasons for
withholding or hiding from her what the lens
so patently displayed. This amplification
of its damaged twin's simplicity
might well have proved to her that we
were further apart than our convention
pretended or imagined. The glaze
of that magnesium flash had isolated
and advertised that my revealed
leering's direction was all for Agnes,
queen of that night's misrule, her mouth
only recently emptied of her hints to me
of her flesh's willing availability.
There had been lewdness in her uncouth
offers and crude anticipations
of the uses I might have of her body,
suggestions whispered quietly
of how I might give her both gratification
and her revenge. My visible intent
was bursting for her, for me easily

the randiest and now most readily
available of the women present,
who, as we danced, had salaciously
offered me more than I knew how
to take from her flesh. I was callow
and a woman had never spoken to me
in such terms, priming expectation
and suggesting the uses I might have
of her body. It was beyond my naïve,
though tarnished innocence, that a woman
would ever use such curious coquetry
or make the proposals she had so calmly,
so tantalisingly and with such crudity.
tricked out in her flesh pledges to me.
By touch, by eye and by voice she promised
a readiness to move a dance more urgent.
The evidence of her availability lay latent
and licentious in my eyes and seemed
unmissable and unmistakable….

7. Aftermath

1.

'It seems a long time since we were dancing.'
She didn't say it but I knew by then
that that or some more recent version
would be the theme to sanitise our meeting.
It had, weighed and found wanting in time,
been a paltry business between us.
Her urgent and erotic whispers
while we were dancing was in need of some
expiation more than explanation.
We needed a code, one that might mollify

her offering of herself, the crudity
of it all, her naked expression
of something that years apart had caused me
to understand what she had needed.
Callow, I had failed to comprehend
what hid in her availability.
Later, I recognised I had never been
the source of her excitement but her mere
instrument, for reasons outside pleasure,
to demonstrate a deeper concern.
What at the time I had been foolish enough
to take as her passion for me turned out,
I think, to have its mood, its real root,
in an adultery she had designed as proof
in a direct and unequivocal avenge
of her husband's infidelities. It must never
have been much more than an insincere
disposal of her body and my leverage
towards her ends. Such substance as I
now gave it came from meanings reviewed
in a long retrospect. There was a charade
within an aura of never-again, a wry
pretence of continuing friendship,
bright smiles and certainly no bitterness
in an achievement marking her success
in matters more important than the flip
commodity of sex.....

2.

      ......As I went
towards her, I remembered her appeal
as an attractive and almost beautiful
woman, certainly one whose intent,
in that unambiguous offering

while the music continued, wasn't one
to be turned down, though on reflection,
it was a long time since we were dancing.

3.

'It seems a long time since we were dancing.'
Did she say it or have I invented it?
It was tangible in the room's conceit.
an ambiguity with a depending
intimation, a phrase she knew would be
sufficient as camouflage and code.
And I remembered, as she intended,
a time before the accident when she
had the use of her legs and whispered
her acid recriminations, making it plain
that she was available.'I was happy then,'
she said. I wondered what alchemy had turned
that dross to gold. She had not been happy.
Agnes herself had probably been
at her most unhappy on an occasion
which seemed in distorted memory
to have undergone a transformation
and transubstantiation. Such a material
adjustment of that night's betrayal
caused me to speculate how protean
things are. But it was a time for platitudes.
Whatever mood had been building,
and I remember its infiltration sliding
in snow outside and in the vicissitudes
of the plush room, that either one or both of us
decided to dissipate its danger.
Her prolonged imprisonment must have made her
sensitive to the expectations of others.
'I'm a lonely woman, Jack. But you can tell me

45

I was attractive. Say I was worth a glance....
just to please me...that you fancied me once.'
She spoke self-mockingly to imply
her retreat. But there had been tears in her eyes
wearing the whiteness of reflected snow.
What she spoke was an ambiguous echo
of our evanescent truths and lies.
Her glance fell to the splayed disarray
of the romances under her chair.
'I'm lonely, Jack. There's only Ellen here.
I could do with better company
than a big, coarse girl...'

8. Ambiguities

Ellen eyed me sourly. She carried a grenade
of the sort I'd seen often enough before,
some relic of the armaments of the moor.
It had been flattened and abraded
and through its centre a widened hole,
that held the coloured spills behind the bar.
'I know you couldn't have phoned from here.'
She set it down between us, her solid symbol
of our difference. 'And Agnes says she wants
to tell you something important.' She spoke
facing the mirror, inventing some speck
on its surface. Between those incidents
I learned the source and substance of her quarrel
and saw my spoiling of the life she shared
with Agnes. I wondered how she'd heard
or guessed the knotted history of all
that nearly happened. The hand-grenade
stood now ironic for new distance,
and carried a more complex resonance
than I'd supposed. 'Not in here,' she said,

'Never in here.' New ambiguities
veiled her warning. 'And I'd be hesitant.
Don't say too much. These days she doesn't want
reminders of your little secrecies…'

9. Witching

1.

'What in hell …' The lights were out. In those
first seconds it was bewildering.
'What bloody fool….'what 's happening…'
I understood it clearly. The darkness was
my own, intentional and set to continue.

*'I know you couldn't have phoned from here.
She loved you once. Not now. You hurt her.'*

Its mappings were geographies I knew.
There was a sudden flaring and the dousing
of a match, a wavering point of redness
experiential in my blackout cosmos.
And then another match, its quick scraping
lighting in that uncertain matrix,
a candle, and in its early splutter,
a halo of radiance no whiter
or wider than a face. As the wick's
osmosis fed the flame, its expansion
lit different dimensions. And by then
I had expected it. I had long reason
to weigh its persisting accusation.

*'You couldn't have phoned from here. You thought
she'd still be yours. Not now. No longer.'*

47

It was then I saw the lank shock of hair,
the bottle-bottom glasses perching the white
moon of his face, his spindle legs and knew
our prolonged acquaintance. In one hand
the candle waved and smoked. The other held
a darkness supporting the pin-prick glow.
Certain that this could never be more
than trickery, my memory's travel
groped in seconds to that original
and witched hallucination of the moor,
Who else would know my landscapes? Only
the inside of a poem. Only one other.

You know you couldn't have phoned from here.
Couldn't you see she's mine? Can't you see why...'

At that time I was convinced the shapes
could be no more than the candle's conjure,
apparitions shaped by the wax's gutter
in fickle air. They were my landscapes,
my inward history. My mind hunted
the secrets of their mirage manufacture.
Bottle-glasses flashed, the flame's glimmer
moved on the moon of face and reached
the white, stalks of legs. I guessed it
to be paltry and contrived, could see
the gist of what had been so cunningly
vouchsafed me. My golem boy twisted
and dissolved. The candle's trick presented
what I had known to expect. Within
the flame's guttering aureole my demon
had laid his gift. I saw the serrated
groovings of latitude and longitude
shaping the segmentation, that defined
its pregnant bulk. I watched its lighted

intensity grow to invoke a crude
and feeble spluttering. In the rank reward
of that spilling, he came again, came ghastly
from the witched past, came towing to me
the fierce moralities of punctured
 and penetrated flesh. 'Dead,' he was shouting,

'You couldn't have phoned from here. You lied.
You lied to me. You lied to her. You tried...'

I knew then the sources of this witching.
The twitch of spark became a fountain,
a scintilla flame and in the lull
of its extinction, I waited the spill
of the inevitable explosion.
Then it came. Not the reverberation
that startled the crescent larks and
moved loaded through the moor's hinterland:
this time, only the squib detonation,
the flare of a penny firework. I reached
towards it, warm from its petty swell
and questioned who could have known so well
the footpaths and landscapes of my mind.
Only myself. The inside of a poem.

'You couldn't have phoned from here. You thought
she'd still be yours. She's mine. Your sort...'

I held the metal docile in my palm,
traced its familiar serrations knowing
its mercator projections of another weight.
I knew it well. Ellen had carried its regret
through sunlight towards me, flaunting
its sour history. Time to recognise
that long since I had elected waste,

49

had chosen the corrupted past,
my self-deceptions, my eroding lies.

2.

'...*tarnishes.*' Always I had moved
on maps of my own need. Each broken wall
and dead encampment had its footpaths plain,
was mythic to my route and fundamental
in all my journeys. On her I had drawn
marches of familiar landscape,
an arid terrain that I knew and when
its features were assembled, they would shape
a whole cartography of upland pain.

10. A tartan blanket

1.

'Come in, Jack.' Agnes's voice was clear.
The remembered tang that I'd encountered
with suspicion in the bar below had
followed me. On the table beside her,
her drink seemed the same as my own.
An ornate clock ticked loudly and slowly.
A tartan, some clan I couldn't identify,
covered her lower half. The collection
of paperback romances seemed the same
as I remembered. 'Is the fog still there?
It caused me to cross to the window where
heavily lined curtains filled the frame,
to draw them slightly and to look out
where the moor might have been. The whole place
was insulated, immured by fog that was
swirling heavily and seemed to butt

less than softly at the glass, turning
the room into a commodious limbo.
of uncertainty. I stared into
that repudiating blankness hearing
Agnes readjust her position.

2.

When I turned, she sat more straightly,
the cast of her face and features strangely
altered and modified. The tartan
was lower around her waist. Lamplight
had failed to soften features which, though stress
had drawn them, were not malicious.
Now the room's subdued lighting had brought
a beak-like hardening and deepening
a skin-tightened quality to her face,
reshaping the hollows of her eyes.
'It seems a long time since we were dancing.'
I had expected it. The air was
pregnant with it. Once there had seemed to be
a plangent, albeit hopeless quality
in the timbre of her tone and voice.
But this was very different, mocking
and ironic. Curtains that had failed
to fall completely together revealed
the mist's corruption infiltrating
our mutual disloyalties before
the accident that took her legs away,
cursing with a sour implacability
her husband's infidelities, sore
for revenge. Somewhere, time was astray.
'It seems a long time since we were dancing.'
I did not know if this were mere repeating,
or if her words had jumped in such a way

51

that I was hearing a new and unsaid
meaning. There were entwined presences,
last time and this time, in its occurrences,
moods past and present with a delayed
and ominous echo. It might be that
neither was said. Lamplight's disorder
had dissolved her features' contour.

3.

I was no longer sure that the tartan blanket
was the one she had been wearing when
I first entered, or changed surreptitiously
while I looked out towards the moor. She
had moved back into one I had known
in our younger days. It lay lower
and looser on her, seemed that it might
almost fall from its covering. The white
blouse she wore closed to her throat before
had opened lower buttons. The light
from the lamp beside her, unequivocal
touched now on the half-revealed swell
of her breast. What seemed a jeune coquette
had replaced her. I noticed only then
that the lipstick she wore was garishly
daubed in a colour almost certainly
years out of date, a gauche girl's fashion
and not a woman's make-up. Its smear
in the corner of her mouth made her seem
pathetic. 'Those years ago, that time,
on that night,' she said, 'I came so near
to loving you...' I remembered then
only the aura of her planned revenge to sting
her husband, and myself the willing,
mechanism. The clock had jerked on.

4.

The coquette, this lipsticked compromise
of past and present, of girl and woman
sat before me. Time had shuddered again.
'Could you make love to me tonight?' This
was the doll and never Agnes speaking.
I could not be sure that the puppet lips
before me had been moved except by the slips
in some long and invisible string,
I looked at the unnatural creature
before me, her shuddering outline
awaiting some form of resolution
and knew then that the mood of the moor
had followed to torment me. Shadows danced
where there was no possibility
of their movement 'Am I so ugly?
Do I frighten you? I didn't frighten you once,
did I? You were greedy for me then.
I still have my needs. I'm playing the tart
and shaming myself, Jack, asking for that,
You wanted me then. I've not forgotten ...'

5.

I could not be certain of the unresolved
images before me. The puppet lips moved
out of sequence with the words. I heard
the pendulum's slow swing. Time stuttered.
The clock's works had slipped, its ratchets
rattled another dimension. This might be
another of those weird and visionary
moments on the fell. Sun was bouncing its
old splendour on the moor's hinterland,
new bracken burgeoned the fell's awakening.

Like a screen shuddering in its searching
for programmed order, vibrating to find
its intended image. Like something seen
through moving water, time readjusted
me Lazarus to revivify the dead.
'Tell me about Joe Anderson again.'
It came suddenly and without reason,
the innocent bathos of that day, that girl,
my lying tales in sunshine unrepeatable.
And with her came the explosion
volleying through the moor with its enduring
reverberation. Black larks came with her
in territories more than familiar
and bleak. *Dead,* someone was shouting.

6.

Now the tartan blanket was the one that
when I entered had been wrapped close
about her waist and the white blouse
was chaste and fastened to her throat.
The curtains at the window were closed,
had never been opened. Paperback romances
were piled alongside the valances
of her chair. It seemed we had moved
from the extremes of the imagined past
to the banalities of the present
and yet there remained some remnant
between us, lying inert but not yet lost
among the plush carpets, the room's stilled shadows,
the fake inn windows of the lampshades
beaming their icon of a simpler world's
domestic cheer. Something curious
had happened between us and she was
determined to ignore it. We had mouthed

its parts and in its necessities performed
the gestures that something numinous
had demanded. I was now more certain
of the present we had distorted,
the writhing echoes of the past that had moved
between us. 'I've been a lonely woman.
Sometimes I forget myself,' she said,
'and say more than I mean.' Her eyes fell
to the paperbacks. The clock's travel
ticked normality. Shadows insisted
that they had never moved, could not have moved.
'It seems a long time since we were dancing.'

Rufus

('Their witches sham death in delusion or delirium. This state they call *Walking in smoke* and believe their souls fly from them to float the stars or rampage in some devil's satellite..')

1. At The World's End

Rufus, outlandish, platyrrhine swung
in a cage spanning a window bay,
a gymnast enclosed, performing
against a moorland spawning a grey
light clawing ravenous at the glass.
Lulled by a thermostat, supple limbs
played tropical against a foliage
of rushes and bare gritstone climbs.
Heretic heat one spidered night seduced
him to renegade. The moon's allure
garbled lost creeds of luxury and urged
escape to the cobwebbed continent of moor.
We found him mummified to gargoyle
within an overhang of shale and grit.
The famished inquisition of the fell
put to the question. Prehensile death
fixed the exotic leafage of his myth
in shrivelled contours. Spiders on the slope
membraned him, webbed him apostate,
stilled the dissent of an infertile hope.

2. Raptors

Fog thinly laminate on tarmac
broke at the car's buffet. The owl

dropped out of darkness in heraldic
headlong, a raptor's swoop to kill
its chrome reflection, a stuka strike
predatorial into the upthrust
belly of headlights. The famish beak
guided splayed talons through mist.
This was a death matadorial
in its short and ritual ferocity
and conflict of flesh and metal.
Only one bled. Above, a clean sky
diminished the whole affair.
Cold planets skidded a moonless vault.
Stars arched imperial to concur
such happenings as the universe's fault
where predators collided in a friction
of competing energies. They were
mere accidents of light and misdirection
made treacherous by chrome's mirror.
Machineries of flesh and metal's innocence
had found their absolute in predatory
collision, the raptor's necessary lance,
the pistons' robotic anarchy.

3. Double Vision

The World's End stood once nameless,
modest, whitewashed within the acid
greens of the fell. Once, in the arcades
of my young ignorance, it held
bright April sunshine, cloud shadow scudding
the reviving rumours of the moor,
scouring in knuckle outcrops, waking
the threadbare grasses. The World's End wore
my virgin landscapes, crowded the vault
bursting with larks. Gaunt poles ran,

quitting the road to file a thin assault
on the white walls. And then that burgeon
left me. Now, in darkness, bitten by
the headlights' mince, that once region
paraded a gilded whore, wantonly
scraping allure's diminished invitation.
Gaudy illumination spilt the name:
bulbs spat their bauble into mist.
Someone shouted 'Rufus'. At the time,
it meant nothing. Among the waste
of stars, one shuddering planet,
a clack of mindless laughter puncturing
the alien polish of the night.
I knew it then. Something was going wrong.

4. Cages

On the fell's flank, spirals of thin snow
balanced and spilled along the gullies.
That room shared with the bar below
Rufus's view. In her commodious
and like imprisonment, Agnes said,
'A long time since we were dancing.' She stirred,
leglessly reasserting what remained
of her once agile self. Open curtains bared
where blanched barrenness of the fell,
echoed our past's emptiness. Easy to guess
that double frisson and our once double
treacheries, our cages' invalidities.
I remembered her whole and beautiful,
cursing her husband and implacable,
it seemed then, to compound and seal
a time when we had danced together. 'Tell
Hughie,' she said, 'that Rufus frightens me.
I'd like that monkey gone. I know that he'll

listen to you.' But she had grown
sensitive in her crippled sentence there,
guessing me loth to try with real conviction.
Again, my lies were bringing back to her
the cages of the past. 'I'll do my best
 Just as before, nothing would come of it.
It was a long time since we danced.
Tears touched her eyes reflecting white
snow trapped and whirling in gullies.
'I've been a lonely woman since –' Eyes were
dropped to the paperback romances
imprisoned, lying beneath my chair.

5. Walking in Smoke

1.

Something was going wrong. Once in the bar,
I walked in smoke. My universe evolved
odours of past deceits, another
moor's infidelities and in that broomride
an agaric otherness possessed me.
A night's mock Sabbat spawned the room,
gaudy and insincere on the witch upland,
wearing the fancy dress of beasts to assume
the prancing of animals. Nearer my mind,
irrational in its buzzing finery,
there came the bulging and prognathous
head of a bluebottle with plastic antennae
shivering my face to waken the mess
of Agnes's boudoir captivity.
Glitter paint shaped the leaning orbit
of multiple eyes. Within that stare
was the malevolence and the implicit

enmity of the basilisk. Fingers were
strumming the mesh of Rufus's prison.
Someone fiddled with the cage's lock,
'Give him his chance to join the fun -'
There was no fun. I walked in smoke
heard again Agnes's pleading, saw
through misted glass behind him,
our once deceits, a whirl of snow
twisting the landscapes of another frame.

2.

Something was going wrong. Again
I walked in smoke. Again my cosmos
evolved the past's deceits, its coven
of broomride infidelities.
Again that agaric otherness
possessed me. My Beelzebub fly
had vanished. That Sabbat's gross
masquerading had left there only
some gaudy tokens of its existence.
The cage's lock was broken. I knelt
before its screech confessor. Rufus
heard mea culpas for promises unkept
and learned the carnal language
that Agnes and myself ingrained,
gibbering no absolution to assuage
atonement's need. Instead, he bit my hand.
It was his ambiguity to be held
both instrument and object of my promise.
A lost smock scarfing my hand, I hauled
doors from his stall and groped to squeeze
his space, to cassock him in the vesture
of that discarded cloth. Once more,
I walked in smoke, unfrocked him at the door,

to bundle his liberty into the moor.

6. Witches

Well, maybe Agnes. Disembodied litter
dressed the car park. A few animal
inventions and a mythic carnivore
grubbed among stones. My bluebottle
Beelzebub flapped antennae, octopus
on a stretched netting. Monstrosity
fluttered, wasting its once disguise
in bushes, its comic commodity
and plastic insincerity now useless,
already disintegrating. The world is
witchless enough and witches anyway,
were always fantasy. And maybe Agnes.
I saw the owl's body where it lay
and heard the land's language. Snow fell on
the inexplicable inscription
of stones: mist spoke the lost religion,
the old knowing. I felt the frisson
of a magic that queried reason's reaches
and groped to learn the planets' alchemies.
The world is witchless enough and witches
never more than fantasy. Or maybe Agnes.

Team Photographs

1. Team Photographs

George led me to the wall where thirtyone
photographs in black and white proposed
thirty one seasons of a side that never won
anything. Young and brash, we colonised
in callow ranks athletically transfixed,
a team without distinction. First, he stared,
not at myself but at Hugh Naylor, relaxed,
arms folded, head erect in an assured
self-confidence in some earlier team.
George spoke, voice loaded with reproach,
'You know the story, that man did me harm.'
He moved to point my later photograph -
'You're sitting where he sat.' - struck visually
to shape our present quarrel. Seasons later, young,
I poised the same null landscape over me,
the slowly vitiating and corroding
townscapes of a time and mood less innocent
than I or our young faces had supposed.
Black and white stripes posed celluloid assent.
Petrified, agonistic, we advertised
different seasons of a side that never won
anything. Upland behind us were
the marches of a landscape I had known,
the blind and narrow town under the moor,
the pattern of the mean, ascending streets
that fashioned us. George pointed Naylor
and myself, wearing corrupting industries,
complicit in that landscape's weather.

2. Some metaphors for the Ground

From a turn in the road, the town lies
camping the moor's flank. Street fingers feel
and grope the fell. Chapel chimneys
tickle its thigh, the jugular canal
arteries through emptied mills. The decayed
white of asbestos stands unleagued
commemorates a side that specialised
in relegation. The pitch preens, grassed
to jewel, in the armpit of this dross
den under the moor. Chapels fail
in bids for re-election: factories
smoke on the transfer list where football
wears faces ripe to move from innocence
in seasons of a side that never won
anything, sliding a limbo dance
from league to league within its worn
tatter of terraces. Folded arms
and fossil grins commemorate a side
- hardened old pros in their last games
and aspirant lads, some of them on the road
to higher leagues - a schizophrenia
matched in results. The white asbestos
leans monument to lost sides that wear
thirty one seasons of a team that tows
its past to swell the grudge offence that sits
the streets and alleyway of this blind
tent under the moor where relegation waits
to stalk us in seasons not yet played.

3. Manager: Arthur Buckley

Manager: Arthur Buckley. It proclaimed
one of lifer's losers. Empty and likeable,
the world's fool, still my friend, unchanged
except his age and girth. He'd stayed the affable
man I remembered. The full-back features,
the swollen, heavy muscles of the neck,
retained their trademark. His body was
fuller but not much clumsier. He took
pride in old photographs damp had spoiled
with emulsions' bombs. Some were past teams,
some, action fragments scissored from old
newspapers, some gripped by blurred frames,
in postures fixing the naivete
that held him gullible, the easy butt
of more worldly games. He could betray
my secret ridicules to grief, a target
making my blame ambiguous for one
of life's persistent losers. *'In this game
for twenty years, what have I ever won?
No medals. Never a cup.'* I pitied him,
not his incompetence or lack of prizes,
but all he never knew, his dull goodness.
His world would need new rules and referees
for him to kiss its cups or wave its trophies.

4. Landlord of The World's End

Our meeting was deliberate enough,
myself and Naylor, near *The World's End*,
his newest strumpet, perching its fief
of moor and car-park. The accident
that scraped his wife to leglessness showed
no scratch on his surface. We climbed to

the moorhead. Beneath us, the town splayed
its legs in the offence of streets we knew,
that shaped simplicity within the space
our ignorance permitted. He spoke
derisively -*'An arsehole of a place'*-
turning to gloat his *World's End's* wantonness
slutting the moor. *'It's mine. I always said
I'd have it. Something sodlike crushes'* -
he pointed -*'our sort down there. I made
certain of better.'* Across the moor
his painted excrescence winked. I guessed
that there Agnes might cuddle the lure,
of paper-back romances. Some malice paced
my own derision. *'How's Agnes been?'*
*'She talks about you, Usually that night
dancing with you. She used to carry on.'*
Despair or some once admiration might
have prompted him. He knew what I had tried.
'There's always Alice, can't be wasted.'
His equal irony brushed aside
my own. *'Which of us is the bastard?'*

5. Four conversations

1. Alice Buckley at The World's End

I knew the mock refinement of her voice
dismissing me as salesman when she said,
'He isn't here -' squawking her compromise
noises, not remembering me. *'Did
Hughie know you were coming? Are you new?'*
The photograph behind her on the wall
was one I'd seen before. On it the row
of losing faces bubbled on a swell
of town and moor, a team on its way

65

to winning nothing. *'Mister Naylor's there -'*
she pointed where he sat. *'He used to play*
for England when he was a footballer.
He's out today.' She queened in his affairs
and thought she knew my business. I knew hers.

2. Landlord of The Dog

'And so, you're back among us -' On his wall,
the serried photographs were spanning
thirty one seasons of a side that fell
steadily through the leagues. Shorts too long
and heavy boots were ranked in black and white,
shirts luminous under the hill.
He nodded to me. *'Hugh Naylor's got*
The World's End now. Tarted it up to pull
the gin trade.' 'Does he get it?' He laughed.
My thought had been the vacant grey
of car park. *'Gets it alright,'* he said.
'A bit more than he should, I've heard. Let's say,
visitors who might be better off
home with their husbands. Your sort of stuff.'

3. Agnes Naylor at The World's End

'And as for Alice, couldn't you see
I've known about her playing his queen.
Couldn't you see I knew?' I saw that she
needed to tell me, had always been
ungulled. *'I'm not so foolish. I've known*
about the others.' I looked for spite,
some spring of sourness in her and saw none.
'His little weakness.' Then I knew that
she hadn't been opponent of his games
but agent and entrepreneur and they

66

were gestures of a sort, her schemes
a kind of love, even compassion.
And then she struck. *'You got your ration.'*

4. Landlord of The Dog

On ruined and recorded landscapes, those
apocryphal photographs still wore
in agonistic, schizophrenic rows,
old disillusion or endeavour.
For his own ironies, he pointed
Buckley and Naylor, team-mates in a side
on the way down. *'You know he's resigned
today? Poor bloody Arthur,'* he said.
'A job for Naylor?' Maliciously,
I fed the snippet to him, let him wind
his answer. *'He does one job for Buckley.
Greedy to give him the other.'* And,
outside irony and unaware,
he was still laughing. I'd had my share.

6. A rhetoric for Naylor's penitence

*'I've had enough of Agnes. You can't tell
what I've put up with.'* Scalding water
that he endured, I found unbearable.
'That whole bloody business with the car -'
He didn't finish or need to finish.
I knew about the car, but better,
its acid preludes. She danced to squash
her sour recriminations in my ear,
resentment fouling the night. Arthur
and Alice Buckley shared the table.
Someone took photographs. Naylor,
quarrelsome, drunk and incapable,

half-killed her on the way home, although
he stayed unscathed. She lost her legs. That was
the business with the car. *'I've had enough,*
it's too much in the end.' In places
penance shower didn't reach, he raised
lather to conceal confessional.
'I want what going but can't get past
Agnes. It's left me with buggerall.
I never wanted more than my ration.
Just some sort of relief and mainly
what you're getting. Alleviation.
My life is skint.' That was his only
occasion of complaint, the one time
I saw the hurt sitting his centre
in loquacious seconds when he came
clean in an assault of scalding water.

7. Those old photographs

'We've had them out. The albums. Old ones -'
Thirteen at table, a white cloth's furl.
a glaze of sharp magnesium hardens
apostle faces. *'Your red-haired girl –'*
Buckley blinks central, haloed by an arch
of window, car headlights on the fell.
His palm lies upward, there is an ash-
tray, wafers and red wine. We smile,
in dresses and suits. Randy Agnes
fixing that flash in virgin white betrays
little except her smirk for Alice
at that strange supper. Her gesture stays.
Naylor leans near Buckley, his pose
mocks innocence. My red-headed girl,
now George's complaint, at that time knows
nothing, though my wafer lust was all

bursting for Agnes. By far the best-
looking, randy and available,
who, when we danced, salacious promised
all that I wanted. Her tongue was full
of spite, jealousy and resentment
tricking her flesh's desire to splay
her readiness for a dance more urgent.
On the drive home, he scraped her legs away,
and that was that, our dancings undone.
All we proposed while smiling behind
the modelled cloth, the wafers and the wine,
the smoking ashtray, never happened.
Captured prophetic, Arthur Buckley
beams innocence where Hugh Naylor
postures the eternal judas-lie.
Alice smiles enigmatic, seems to stare
at truth on or beneath Agnes's dress'
'We've had them out. Old photographs that shame
you at your games. Touching up Agnes,
and that girl you shagged. What was her name?'

8. Housewarming

'No holy water with it?' I'd never known
Naylor to water whisky. *'Where's the tap?*
I'm driving.' I recalled he'd driven
drunker. As children, we'd known the shape
of houses like this, were dough in these
unleavened alleys and knew the cage
of their yards, their rooms' geographies.
His water was charade to camouflage
words for my ear. We measured a bare
space of stone-flagged kitchen. *'Buckley's*
finished. I don't know what they've told her.'
Our host's housewarm laughter cut across

69

his secret. *'If she knows,'* - he eyed the regions
where Alice stood - *'she hasn't said. Cancer.'*
Awed confessional and the kitchen's
cold air penanced it. *'Only a year*
they give him. I hope he never knows.'
Which flesh or whose betrayal he ought
never to know I never knew. The brass
tap spun under his hand. Water spat,
rumbling piped to blur his confession
although he kept his glass well outside
its splutter. *'Some circumstances when*
camouflage matters,' I think he said.

9. Apples for a dying man

'He loves to sit among his apple trees.'
Alice told spreading orchards to cheer
his illness. *'Out in his summer-house.'*
Arthur was watching from his lawn's square
a match of wind and bloom. Six lean trees
were losing badly in an enclosure
of concrete, on that poor pitch, for his
last season's game. Fragile, immature
blossom was being kicked to defeat.
His hair had greyed, his cheeks sunk and thinned,
the bull-neck lost its force. He nodded at
the trees' flimsy bloom. *' If you come round*
a bit later, I'll give you some fruit.'
Wind butting urban sunshine culled
unfruiting seed. Sucking at bottled
stout for his health, he raised his glass to pour
badly, spilling liberal froth that rode
towards the trees. Bottle and flower
conflicted in his mood. *'Guinness is good.*
What did I win but relegation?'

Seen from his shelter, the match had run
to its result. The bitter question
blew from his mouth, like the froth was borne
downwind to join the fallen bloom that.
once promising succulence, now lay
among the dead leaves and the birdshit,
latent to spur a richer life. Maybe.

10. A threnody for dancings done

'It's a long time since we were dancing –'
Agnes cadenced her tentative phrase
towards me, unsure but still causing,
as she had intended to cause,
recall of a time when we had had
hope of a different dancing as we danced.
That night she spent her venom in tirade
condemning Naylor. Now she evidenced
her need that I might still remember
our conspiracy. On the way home,
still angry, he broke the car and her.
It cost her her legs. That quarrelsome
night of our dancing brought back to me
her offers of a more urgent dancing,
recalled her acid mood and finally
her features, finely beautiful, parading
her crudest promises to my ear.
I searched new ironies for a face
once beautiful but now angular,
distorted and that night's ugly voice
the gentlest that I knew. She had been
urgent then, queer lewdness in her tone,
projecting it as her game's design.
And afterwards, as he drove her home,
that cruel, crippling business when

71

he broke the car and her. My thought hung
on the spaces of her life since then.
'It's a long time since we were dancing –'

11. Blackberry and apple pie

'He can have his home-grown apples with them –'
She poured the berries slowly and they ran
like blood in an enamelled sunstream,
pulsed liquid and uncurdled, from one
bag to another. *'Yes, it's cancer.'*
Thin plastic squealed where her fingers fought.
'Blackberry and apple pie.' Her anger
held all malignant nature in garotte.
She screwed the neck, with deliberation
tightened it, to burst the berries' blood.
Ribbons of juice spurted a profusion
for vicious lubricant to her mood.
'With his own apples - 'Jewelled sun lurched
on fruit debauched, bulging as she strained
to scorpion anger where she arched
and stung herself. Under her blenched hand,
swollen and tight, the red membrane burst
to spurt slush fruit. I heard her scream
of anger the distending bag released.
'What use are fucking blackberries to him –'

12. A fireplace with a copper hood

'Tell Naylor I know now.' A tongued fire
was blazing, brawling a copper throat.
His face, reflected, was a skull and wore
a medieval mask of death. A bright
scutter of ash moved firelight within
its indentations. His bitter words
swelled in a metal cheek's emblazon
on moquette. He slid dull eyes towards
team photographs, the lost sides askew
over the hooded fire, where in the line,
himself and Naylor grinned the same spew
of rotting stands. *'What did we ever win?*
It's all a bloody cheat.' Firelight was
scraping a face ridged by the moquette's
impress. *'I know that now.'* His braces
drooped slack to slip frail shoulders. His
trousers gaped where once his belly had
swollen the waist. A bluster of wind
was sucking elastic tongues renewed
from the flat fire. *'Tell Naylor I found*
out in the end.' Which flesh and blood
treacheries he'd solved I never knew.
Such words he howled from that copper hood
were all time's relegations blowing through
poor sides unleagued shaping the bleak
metaphor of narrow streets, the sour
untruths of chapels, the god we make
from images of fear at what we are.

13. Requiem

Thirty one photographs still enshrine
those sides unfutured in their team rows,
screwing to private relegation.
Decaying asbestos stands enclose
the jewel pitch. Mills slouch degenerate
under the moor. Heads erect, arms folded,
agonistic, we commemorate
thirty one seasons of a limbo slide,
thirty one seasons of flesh and blood's
latent treacheries. Buckley's cheer,
if it survives, must simplify sides
in alien leagues. With Naylor,
I share ungrounded fixtures, played
away from home. More than the cameras'
coincidences fix us among greed
mills and chapels where our faces
stare into time not innocent from time
not innocent. We posture the bruised,
legitimate offspring of our noisome
camp on the moor, propose the crude
bible of matches lost in its streets,
acknowledge as our father the god
of games where relegation waits
to stalk us in seasons not yet played.

Mapping the Moor

1.

Maps draw their makers' minds,
chart the spirit's orreries to display
a different ghost. Under the land's
icon lies another geography.

My father's father's Lancashire,
my father's, mine records a sour
religion sucking austere
sustenance from the famine moor.

We knew a barren contour
of tight lips. Our maps sanction
no legend for the ardent or
lexicon for his death's occasion.

2.

On his old maps, curlews
named moorland over soot Maydays
in mill villages. Delirious,
arching to a remembered cause,

he shouted, *'Where's the accident?'*
No tracks invade that region
or charts presume that continent.
How do you tell a dying man

he is the accident? Precise
cartographies of the real
encode within their geographies
a shuddering spiritual.

On my new maps, Mercedes
commuters tart mill cottages
in the moor. Geographies
unchanged wear shifted images.

3.

I mean our maps. A map dances
its maker's mind, sings somewhere
within its graphic assurances,
the spatial fables of another

and ineffable territory.
he said, *'I'm not much use at dying,
I've never done it before.'* In my
museum of charts, I hang

that ultimate cartography
of flesh's dependency, the bleak
boundaries of eternity
encompassed in a stale joke.

4.

A blackened psalm-box heaving
harmonium bleaknesses
and hymnal caterwauling
into my moor wrangles its place

on all our maps. Within its cramp
marshalling yard, the menhir
regiments and the sooted pomp
of grocers' obelisks require

reveille's bugle where the fell's
bleak code and barren signature
ethic the self-denials
implicit in our contour.

And once, in sudden sunlight,
during alchemies of sleet,
I saw its prison railings bright
as a necklace of marcasite.

My father's father's Lancashire.
my father's, mine, records a sour
contagion mapping austere
apocrypha on our famine moor.

We sanctified a parable
of tight lips. Our maps' custom
denied a lexicon or scale
or language for love's idiom.

I mean a map. My map dances
its maker's mind, incarnate, rants
within its graphic assurances,
fables attempting sustenance.

5.

I mean a map. But how translate
the heart to flattened landscape?
This was a quarry grief and that
some outcrop pain. Can any map

encompass and hold retrievable
in paper correlatives,
the feint, uncopiable
lattices whose grid contrives

labyrinths in dimensions
that have no northings, eastings,
the transubstantiating zones
of the mind's rememberings?

I mean a map more than cartoon
similes and simulation.
But by what logarithm can
the heart's countries be known?

How make a chart so integral
that, subliminal, it maps
the making of itself, and all
shifting allegiances and shapes

lie esemplastic in its scheme?
I mean maps: lost parables
of barren farms, forgotten intake's
apocrypha, that sour religion's

anathema. I mean a map
whose arcane undertaking
is parthenogenesis, whose trope
the guile of its own making.

6.

It is my map, but how to say
his dying moved me? Not the death
but the self's seismology
metamorphic within its myth.

My father's father's Lancashire,
my father's, mine, nurtured the sour
osmotic autisms that were
the instinct language of our moor.

We traded barren contours
of tight lips. Our maps deny
the ostentation of remorse,
the luxuries of threnody.

I scrawl a map above a map.
He said, *'I'm not much use at dying,
I've never done it before.'* This shape
I scheme on cellophane to bring

another map beneath and see,
by lineage or the chance
of duplicate geography,
an imposed equivalence.

'Why are they always,' she said,
such hostile landscapes?' She meant,
skirting the moor, the crowded
fables under us, the immanent

apostasies of the past.
I draw that map. The parables
of spent workings: the manifest
of ruins: the runes of broken walls.

And sometimes, jewelled sunlight
transmuting a thunder rain
has conjured dearth's palatinate
to the landscapes of Cockaigne.

7.

On his old maps, curlews
named moorland over lost Maydays
in mill villages. Mine pursues
a shifting weather's ironies.

I make a map of time, one wry
and existential second stilled.
In it, on flat-cap holiday,
charabanc mashers are held

in equipoise, soot calyxes
of blossom seize in an opulent
embalming. Memory fixes
that howl of *'Where's the accident?'*

where simian, in oriental
attitudes of carved bone,
caged monkeys, for gawp's festival,
are staring tarsier from stone.

Fermata strangles the band's
tuba kazoo. Spring's anthem
of larks in the moor's hinterlands
is hushed. In sunlight's stratagem,

the swingboat's stayed pelota,
straining at counterpoise,
preserves the stilled parabola
of its compliant prejudice

with death. Somebody's Woodbine
droops unlit. Somewhere a silent
palaver boils and someone
is shouting *'Where's the accident?'*

A boat upturned farts sucker-cup
in the mill lodge's frame. Lost oars
skulk crocodile. On the bank slope,
a keyboard of drowned flesh infers

that bright day's gothic havoc.
Then larks rage unfrozen. The swingboat
remembers its plunging arc.
The monkeys scratch their fleas. That shout

encodes its semiotic shriek
in a prism hiatus
where being resumes its antic
and clockwork nothingness.

On my new maps, Mercedes
commuters are tarting barns
in the mill villages. The past's screes
weather to capital's religions.

I chart an ironic anguish,
a map less to mean than be,
whose metaphor stalks language
for its implicit geology.

8.

It is my map. Secret in my
chartroom's hangings, there is
that Chapel's long apostasy
carved in the soft integrities

of a living cell. Etched in
a dying mind's integument
is that Mayday mayhem: someone
is shouting, *'Where's the accident?'*

Deeply scrimshawed into bone
are landscapes of spent industries,
rank farms, the failing benison
of lime in intake's bitterness.'

'Why, always for you,' she said,
'are they hostile landscapes?' She meant
the moor's immanence, the crowded
apocrypha of its taint.

The marshalled menhirs of a yard
necklaced in iron wait display.
Obelisk alleys are scored
intaglio on a dry eye.

We traded in a religion
of tight lips and knew no chart
for subtler exploration
of the geographies of the heart.

I mean a map whose contours
flex esemplastic, yoking
compacted doctrines to enforce
the textures of its own making.

I mean a map. My map stutters
its maker's mind, lisps somewhere
within its coded structures,
its apprehension of a queer

and more arcane peninsula.
He said, *'I'm not much use at dying.
I've never done it before.'* In a
museum of joke charts, I hang

that ineffable region
of flesh's state, the wry acrostic
of nowhere, dry-point within
my doubting dialectic.

Monkey business

1.

'Is that you, Jack?' The telephone's clatter
had jolted me from sleep. The night's mist
had burned to a thin sunlight. Naylor's interest
would be his own affairs. 'Some silly bugger
let Rufus out. Broken his cage. I could name
somebody who'll be pleased to see him lost.'
Agnes lay under his tongue. My first
concern had been for her, her part in the game
of their marriage. I dressed unwillingly.
My head ached. Driving into the fell,
pale sunshine fretted conditional
on the moor's reaches. Where the road runs awry,
swerving to avoid an intruding coign,
there was the feathered wreckage of an owl
and, for seconds, a wings-wide kestrel
hung in the wind's twisting distortion.

2.

In the empty car park, Naylor had waited
my driving there, a coffee steaming
between gloved hands. Last mist was clearing
from the fell's dome swelling acid
in sunlight behind his shoulder. A thin
column of smoke was stringing his chimney
to brighter air above. 'I needed somebody...'
His porch was strung with an unbroken chain
of webs, stray filaments glistening, billowing
in a freshening wind. At the car park's corner,
party streamers, snakes slithering the moor,

fluttered and writhed, striking at nothing,
from where, further down their coil,
wind failed to break flimsy adherence
to drying asphalt. One spiralled sudden menace,
sidewinding into grass. 'Some bloody fool
cracked open his cage, and forced the bloody lock...'
Behind the building the day's kestrel hung,
bracing to stoop in a shuddering
stasis. 'No help in that direction.' His look
implied the undrawn curtains of Agnes's room.
Snakes moved with him, to breach the spiders'
entrapments. It was a day for predators.

3.

'I know what we're doing is useless, but...'
I saw no likelihood but followed him, coursing
from right to left of him and slowly searching,
though hardly diligently and without
much hope, among the skirt concealment
of gullies. Naylor was over the crest
and out of sight, his detective zest
leading him into the moor. My own hunt
took in the marshes behind the building.
I knew it useless, no more than gesture
within the game between us. Seeping water
and rushes were models for the overhang
latent between us. Brackish rivulets ran
through compacted shale. A fickle
sunshine flickered in marches over the pale
mesh of the moor. It must have been then
I saw the kestrel 's hovering question,
riding intently in some slow compass
of stiller air, poising in a hiatus
of recognition and sharp rejection.

Expecting nothing, I scrambled to reach
and rout within fringed edges of shale.
Naylor was waving semaphore, some signal
conveying the hopelessness of our search
My eyes re-shaped the camouflage beneath
the kestrel's interest. Rufus lay knotted
and shrivelled there. Spiders had shrouded
his foetus folding. More than a monkey's death
was with me then. Something waited. Tensions
inhabited the closing space between us,
a latent and electrical unease,
the intensity of unspoken questions.

4.

I let Rufus lie but signalled Naylor
urgently towards me. He came quickly,
loose shale slipping under him in the gully,
dropping his pace, unbalanced and unsure
of his footing before he stooped and reached
into the fronds to loosen the creature,
scraping the webs from congealing fur
and totally unaffected. 'Stupid little sod.'
Once on the moor, I wondered what he saw
or won from that shrivelled homunculus.
Then suddenly, unprovoked, impetuous,
and in an elastic energy, he threw
the body high into the air. I thought,
at first. that he was shaping to volley it
in its descent towards us, but still acute
in his reflexes, at the last moment,
he stayed his movement to catch it in its fall
an inch from the ground. Again in his hand,
the body held its foetal form, unloosened
from the spider's entanglements and soil

of the gully. Once over the ridge, the road
came into sight, the white pub handsome
in an evanescent sunlight under the dome.
In Agnes's window the curtain fluttered.
He turned, sardonic towards me. 'I could name
somebody who'll be glad at what we've found.'
Something waited. Its mood had kestrelled
between us throughout our morning's game.

5.

'I'll tell you this, Jack - 'Our morning's oddity
was stirring him to comment as he dangled
the monkey's corpse from an extended hand –
'I can think of one bugger likely to be
smug about this. She's never fancied Rufus.
But she fancied you, didn't she?' He tossed
the words impishly towards me. Something waited.
Till then, I'd never known how much he'd guess
about that. He answered unspoken questions.
'…of course I knew about it. I closed my eyes,
even then.' He continued to surprise
and disconcert me. In the moor's regions,
sun moved in planes on the fell's dome.
'If only you'd taken her off me then, things might
have been better all round. No accident…'
I knew his guilt, remembered the bloody event,
her broken body after the drunken night.
'And I'd have managed pretty happily
without her. She's been a bitch to me
since then. I would have owed you and she
might have her legs….' The spiders' industry
fluttered broken between pillars of his entry.
Snakes had moved further into the moor.
Ellen, Agnes's keeper stood at the door.

'Jack found him.' He pushed the congealed monkey
towards her. 'In the marshes over the pastures.
This side of the quarry.' She said nothing,
no conventional noises, no gestures
of sympathy, though I was aware
that something strong and tacit lay between them.
She signalled Agnes's open window
and tried to take the monkey from him. 'No,'
she said, 'not that.' It was a scream
and not the voice or tone of a hireling.

6.

He held on to the monkey, spiders' thread
trailing from it, as they played out
a disagreement between equals, one not
between hireling and employer. I recognised
that she had understood his purpose and had
tried to frustrate it. Ellen heard but ignored
my interruption, still meaning to impede
his movement past her through the webs' blockade
'No, Hughie. No. Not that.' She grappled
to take the monkey and stood her ground to hinder
his entry but he shielded Rufus from her.
She had no answer to the feint he made,
lunging wrongly and clumsily for him
while he went to her other side. 'Just stay.
Don't follow him,' she ordered me abruptly,
turning to chase him. There was a scream.
'She won't want you up there till this is over.'
Agnes screamed again from above and Ellen,
a new and raw concern marking her then,
almost the gesture and expression of a lover,
had begun her lumbering climb on the stairs ….

88

7.

We found that conscript monkey in a trench,
sprawled dead, his khaki battledress congealed,
where fallen trucks sheltered his sap advance
into the moorland's shale. A high command,
some inkling instinct of remembered liberty
ordered him breach his cage to march the moor
and soldier in that hostile territory
where trip-wire spiders waited for
the bayonet frost that took him stealthily.
We found him sprawled, a simple fusilier,
ignorant of who had been his enemy
or what the causes of the battle were.
Whatever trumpet called him, whatever drum,
they fibreglassed his mouth to fix him dumb.

Iron and stone contending in the grab
and gouge of quarries wounding the moor
made backdrop to that ending. She tore a web,
complex and labyrinthine as our warfare,
its filaments patterning the cavities
of a wall's decay. Near us, gossamer
linked the rusting trucks. She broke their ties,
numerous as nerves, made metaphor,
in her destruction of their delicacy,
for our disease. Around us and between us,
wrecked membranes of the spiders' industry
told the fragility of webs. Such surgeries
of their transparent, intricate ligament
signalled the warp and weft of our complaint.